JANE GOODALL

BOOK FOR CURIOUS KIDS

Exploring the Extraordinary Life of a Pioneer Scientist Among Her Chimpanzee Companions

ERIC LYLANI

ERIC LYLANI

TABLE OF CONTENTS

INTRODUCTION

Have you ever wondered what it's like to communicate with chimpanzees? Or how these intelligent creatures live, eat, and interact with each other? Join me on an exciting journey into the world of one of the most renowned scientists of our time, Jane Goodall, and her incredible adventures studying chimpanzees in the wild.

Imagine sitting in the dense forests of Africa, surrounded by curious chimpanzees swinging through the trees. What secrets do they hold? What can we learn from their behavior? Get ready to uncover the fascinating life of Jane Goodall and her lifelong dedication to understanding these remarkable creatures.

In this book, we'll embark on a thrilling expedition through Jane Goodall's experiences, from her transformative encounter with a furry friend that sparked her passion to her groundbreaking discoveries about chimpanzee society and her tireless efforts to protect these endangered animals. Each chapter unveils a new aspect of Jane Goodall's extraordinary life and work, offering insights into her adventures, challenges, and triumphs in the pursuit of conservation and understanding.

Get ready to be inspired by Jane Goodall's remarkable journey from secretary to world-renowned chimpanzee scientist. We'll explore the deep bonds of chimpanzee families, the complexities of their language, and the innovative ways Jane has

championed   animal   welfare   and
environmental conservation.

So, grab your curiosity, and let's dive into
the captivating world of Jane Goodall and
her mission to protect chimpanzees and
their habitats. This book is for all the
curious kids who dream of making a
difference and learning more about the
incredible creatures that share our planet.

ERIC LYLANI

A Furry Friend Sparks a Passion

Once upon a time, in the bustling city of London, a little girl named Valerie Jane Morris-Goodall was born in April 1934. Her dad, Mortimer Herbert Morris-Goodall, was a businessman, and her mom, Margaret Myfanwe Joseph, was a talented novelist who wrote under the name Vanne Morris-Goodall. Jane's family was not like everyone else's—they had a special love for adventure and storytelling.

As a young girl, Jane's family moved to the picturesque seaside town of Bournemouth, where the salty breeze and crashing waves became the backdrop of her childhood. Here, Jane attended Uplands School, a cozy independent school nestled in nearby Poole. Even at a young age, Jane's heart was brimming with curiosity about the natural world.

One day, Jane's father gave her a most unusual gift—a stuffed chimpanzee named Jubilee. This wasn't your typical teddy bear! Jubilee had a mischievous grin and bright eyes that captured Jane's imagination. While some of her mother's friends worried that the toy might frighten her, Jane was enchanted. Jubilee quickly became her closest companion, sparking her deep love for animals.

In Jane's room, Jubilee held a place of honor on her dresser, a constant reminder of her passion for the wild and wonderful creatures of the world. Jane would spend hours with Jubilee, imagining herself exploring distant jungles and discovering new animal friends.

Little did Jane know that her early adventures with Jubilee were just the beginning of an extraordinary journey. Her childhood fascination with animals would lead her to the wilds of Africa, where she would become one of the most famous animal experts the world has ever known.

Today, in Jane's home in London, Jubilee still sits on her dresser—a cherished relic from a time when a young girl's curiosity and a simple stuffed chimpanzee sparked a lifelong love affair with the natural world.

ERIC LYLANI

Tarzan's Influence

Jane was not like most other girls her age. While they played with dolls and talked about princesses in fairy tales, Jane preferred something different—adventures in the wild.

One day, Jane stumbled upon a set of old books in her grandmother's attic. The pages were yellowed, and the covers were worn, but the stories inside were bursting with excitement. These were the tales of Tarzan, the Lord of the Jungle.

In the books, Tarzan was a remarkable character—a boy raised by apes in the heart of Africa. His parents, English nobles, were stranded on the west coast of Africa when he was just a baby. Left alone in the jungle, Tarzan was adopted and raised by a tribe of great apes. He grew up swinging through trees, communicating with animals, and defending his jungle home from danger.

As Jane devoured each page, she found herself transported into the depths of the African wilderness. The descriptions of towering trees, exotic animals, and the calls of chimpanzees awakened something deep within her—a longing to explore this untamed world.

"Imagine living among the apes," Jane would say dreamily as she lay under the shade of a tree, her mind wandering to distant lands.

The more Jane read about Tarzan's adventures, the more her desire to visit Africa grew. She yearned to experience the sights, sounds, and smells of the African forests described in the books. The stories sparked her imagination and filled her dreams with visions of swinging through vines and encountering wild creatures.

Jane began to imagine herself as part of Tarzan's world. She envisioned herself befriending chimpanzees, learning their ways, and living in harmony with nature. Her passion for the wild world blossomed with every turn of the page.

One evening, while watching the sunset from her bedroom window, Jane made a silent promise to herself. "One day," she whispered to the evening breeze, "I will go to Africa and discover its secrets, just like Tarzan."

ERIC LYLANI

From Secretary to Chimpanzee Scientist

Jane Goodall's journey into the world of animals and Africa began when she visited a farm in the Kenya highlands in 1957. It was there that she met a friend who would change her life forever.

Jane decided to stay in Africa and found work as a secretary. Her friend suggested she call Louis Leakey, a famous archaeologist and scientist who studied ancient human history. Jane didn't know it at the time, but Louis Leakey was looking for someone to study chimpanzees—the closest living relatives to humans—to learn more about our ancestors.

Louis Leakey was impressed by Jane's passion for animals. Instead of hiring her as a secretary, he sent her to Olduvai Gorge in Tanzania to study chimpanzees. This was the start of Jane's incredible journey into the wild world of primates.

In 1958, Louis Leakey arranged for Jane to travel to London to study primate behavior and anatomy. Jane learned everything she could about these amazing creatures from experts like Osman Hill and John Napier.

Finally, in 1960, Jane set off for Gombe Stream National Park in Tanzania. She was joined by her mother, who was there to make sure they stayed safe in the wild. Jane's mother always supported her dreams, especially at a time when women were not often welcomed into scientific fields.

Jane's groundbreaking work studying chimpanzees in their natural habitat paved the way for other women to pursue careers in science. Over the years, more and more women have followed in Jane's footsteps, thanks to her courage and determination.

In 1962, Louis Leakey helped Jane enroll at the University of Cambridge to study for her PhD, even though she didn't have a bachelor's degree. Jane became the eighth person ever allowed to do this at Cambridge!

Jane worked hard and completed her thesis on the behavior of free-living chimpanzees in 1966. Her research revolutionized our understanding of these incredible creatures.

In 2006, Jane received an honorary Doctor of Science degree from the Open University of Tanzania, celebrating her lifetime of dedication to studying and protecting animals.

Overcoming Obstacles

In 1960, at the age of 26, Dr. Goodall embarked on a groundbreaking mission in Tanzania's Gombe National Park to study chimpanzees. Armed with a high school education, a passion for animals, and her mother by her side, she faced an immense task: find, observe, and record the behavior of wild chimpanzees.

However, things didn't go smoothly at first. Despite her enthusiasm, Dr. Goodall struggled to observe the chimpanzees up close. Thick forests, steep valleys, and dense undergrowth made it difficult to get near the chimps without scaring them away.

For weeks, Dr. Goodall and her team trekked through the park, hoping to catch a glimpse of their elusive subjects. But the chimpanzees were wary and elusive, fleeing whenever they sensed human presence.

To make matters worse, Dr. Goodall and her mother fell ill with malaria. As they battled the illness, time was running out. With only three months of funding left, Dr. Goodall faced a critical point in her research.

Then, one day, a breakthrough. From a distance, Dr. Goodall spotted three chimpanzees calmly observing her. Encouraged by this interaction, she continued her observations and finally had a chance to closely observe a group of chimpanzees feeding on fig trees.

"It was by far the best day I had since my arrival at Gombe," Dr. Goodall recalled. This pivotal moment marked the turning point in her study.

Dr. Goodall's journey teaches us that science is not always straightforward. It's filled with challenges and setbacks. But with perseverance and determination, she overcame these obstacles and made groundbreaking discoveries about chimpanzee behavior.

Insights into Chimpanzee Life

In 1960, Jane Goodall began an extraordinary adventure studying chimpanzees in Gombe Stream National Park, Tanzania. She was curious about these fascinating creatures and wanted to learn more about their lives.

Jane discovered something amazing—chimpanzees are a lot like us! They have their own personalities, thoughts, and feelings of joy and sadness. Jane observed chimpanzees hugging, kissing, patting each other on the back, and even tickling, just like humans do. These gestures showed the strong bonds of love and support within their families and communities, which can last for over 50 years.

But Jane's discoveries didn't stop there. She challenged two big ideas of her time. Many people believed only humans could make and use tools and that chimpanzees were vegetarians. However, Jane saw a chimpanzee named David using blades of grass to "fish" for termites—a clever trick to get a tasty snack! Other chimpanzees made tools by stripping leaves from twigs to make them more effective for grabbing food.

These findings amazed everyone, including Jane's mentor, Louis Leakey. He joked that they might have to redefine what it means to be human if chimpanzees were using tools, too!

Despite their loving side, Jane also witnessed the wild nature of chimpanzees. They would team up to hunt and eat smaller monkeys like colobus monkeys. Jane watched as they cleverly trapped a monkey in a tree and then shared the catch with their troop.

Jane's discoveries changed the way scientists understood chimpanzees. They are not just like us emotionally, but they also use tools and have complex social behaviors. Jane's work showed that chimpanzees are more like us than anyone had imagined, and her adventures continue to inspire us to learn about and protect these incredible animals.

ERIC LYLANI

Joy and Struggle in the Jungle

In the jungle of Gombe, Jane Goodall witnessed not only the loving and playful side of chimpanzees but also their darker behaviors. She saw that dominant females would sometimes harm the young of other females in the troop to keep their own power. This was shocking to Jane because she had thought chimpanzees were mostly kind creatures. But just like humans, chimpanzees had a hidden side that could be quite brutal.

Jane wrote about a difficult time called the Gombe Chimpanzee War in her book "Through a Window: My Thirty Years with the Chimpanzees of Gombe." This war showed how much like humans, chimpanzees could be, but in a much darker way.

Jane did something special in her studies. Instead of giving numbers to the chimpanzees, as other scientists did, she gave them names. This made her bond with them even stronger. In fact, she became so close to the chimps that she was accepted into their society and lived among them as the lowest-ranking member for almost two years!

Among the chimps Jane named were David Greybeard, a friendly male who first trusted her; Goliath, a bold alpha male; Mike, a clever chimp who became the new leader; Humphrey, a big and tough male; Gigi, a gentle "aunt" to young chimps; Mr. McGregor, a grumpy elder; Flo, a caring mother with her children Figan, Faben, Freud, Fifi, and Flint; and Frodo, Fifi's strong and aggressive son who unfortunately made Jane leave the troop when he became the alpha male.

Jane's discoveries showed that chimpanzees are complex creatures with their own personalities and relationships, just like us. Her courage and dedication to understanding these animals continue to inspire people around the world.

ERIC LYLANI

Meeting David Greybeard

In the dense forests of Gombe National Park, Jane Goodall embarked on an incredible journey to study chimpanzees. Little did she know, her life was about to change forever when she encountered a wise and gentle chimp named David Greybeard.

Jane arrived at Gombe full of curiosity and excitement. She was determined to learn about the secret lives of chimpanzees. But as she ventured deeper into the forest, the chimpanzees remained elusive. They were wary of this unfamiliar human in their midst.

One day, as Jane sat quietly beneath a towering fig tree, she heard rustling in the branches above. Peering up, she caught a glimpse of a magnificent chimp with a silvery beard. It was David Greybeard.

David seemed curious about Jane, so he cautiously approached her. His eyes held a mixture of caution and intrigue. Jane remained still, watching David with wonder.

To break the ice, Jane offered David a banana. At first, David hesitated, unsure of this human's intentions. But when he tasted the sweet fruit, a bond began to form between them.

Day after day, Jane returned to the fig tree, accompanied by her newfound friend. David introduced her to his chimpanzee family, showing her their playful antics and intricate social interactions.

One afternoon, Jane witnessed something extraordinary. David picked up a slender twig and carefully stripped off its leaves. With precision, he used the twig to fish for termites in a mound. This was the first time Jane had ever seen a chimpanzee use tools.

David Greybeard's actions amazed Jane. She realized that chimpanzees were more intelligent and resourceful than anyone had imagined.

Over time, David and Jane developed a deep bond of trust. He allowed her to observe intimate moments within the chimpanzee community, from tender mother-child interactions to playful displays of affection.

David Greybeard became a symbol of Jane's pioneering work. His gentle nature and intelligence inspired Jane to continue her research, unraveling the mysteries of chimpanzee behavior.

David Greybeard was Dr. Jane Goodall's favorite chimpanzee and the first individual at Gombe to trust Jane. With his distinctive silver facial hair, David was not only a tool user but also the first chimpanzee Jane observed eating meat.

David was not only a close friend to Dr. Goodall but also a companion to his fellow chimpanzee, Goliath. Often, David comforted Goliath by placing a hand on his head or body, especially when Jane observed the two chimpanzees. He exhibited great tolerance and kindness, maintaining a gentle temperament even when others became aggressive.

In addition to teaching Dr. Goodall about primate behavior, David also assisted her by introducing other chimpanzees when he visited her camp. Without David's helpful introductions, Jane might not have been able to meet the other chimpanzees of Gombe.

Jane believes that David Greybeard died during a pneumonia outbreak in 1968. Time Magazine designated David as one of the 15 most influential animals to have ever lived.

David Greybeard's legacy continues to inspire researchers and conservationists around the world, showcasing the remarkable intelligence and social complexity of chimpanzees.

ERIC LYLANI

Fifi and Her Chimp Family

In the lush forests of Gombe National Park lived a remarkable chimpanzee named Fifi. Fifi wasn't just any chimpanzee—she was the matriarch of her chimp family, a group that Jane Goodall studied closely for many years.

Fifi, born in 1958, was the only daughter of Flo, another influential chimp in Jane's research. Over the years, Fifi grew to become a dominant matriarch herself, leading her family with wisdom and strength. She gave birth to nine offspring: Freud, Frodo, Fanni, Flossi, Faustino, Ferdinand,

Freud (named after his older brother who passed away), Flirt, and Furaha.

When Jane first arrived at Gombe, Fifi was just a curious two-year-old, often riding on her mother's back as they navigated the dense jungle. As Fifi matured, she displayed an energetic and independent spirit. Unlike some chimps who enjoyed socializing, Fifi preferred the company of her mother, Flo, and had few close friends.

Fifi was known for her unique talents, like her exceptional throwing skills, even though her aim was not always accurate. Despite her solitary nature, Fifi was a caring mother and a respected leader within her community.

In August 1990, Dr. Jane Goodall captured a touching moment between Fifi and her infant son, Faustino. This photograph beautifully illustrates the profound bond between mother and child within chimpanzee society. Fifi, assuming the role of alpha female after her mother Flo's passing, emerged as a remarkable leader at Gombe. She became renowned as the most prolific mother among the female chimps, birthing nine times with only two tragic losses in infancy.

Throughout her life, Fifi faced many challenges, including changes in her habitat and encounters with other wildlife. In 2004, Fifi disappeared, and she was soon presumed to have passed away. She was the last surviving chimpanzee at Gombe from Dr. Goodall's early days.

Fifi's legacy lives on in the memories of those who studied her and the lessons she taught about chimpanzee life. Through Fifi's story, we learn about the complexities of chimp society and the bonds that tie families together in the wild.

And so, the tale of Fifi and her chimp family continues to inspire us to cherish and protect these incredible animals and their natural habitats.

Meeting The Mighty Frodo

Deep in the heart of Gombe National Park, among the lush green trees and winding paths, lived a legendary chimpanzee named Frodo. Frodo wasn't just any chimp—he was the alpha male, the leader of his chimpanzee family.

Frodo was born on June 30, 1976, to his remarkable mother, Fifi, a successful and respected matriarch in Gombe. From a mischievous little chimp, Frodo grew into a towering alpha male—a strong and fearless leader among his peers.

Jane Goodall, the scientist who studied chimps like Frodo, named him after a character from a beloved story called "The Lord of the Rings." Like the hobbit Frodo from the story, this chimpanzee had a strong and determined spirit.

As Frodo grew older, he became known for his powerful presence and sometimes naughty behavior. He loved to throw rocks and play rough, but he was also a dedicated protector of his chimpanzee community.

In 1997, Frodo achieved the highest honor a chimp could have—he became the alpha male by defeating his own brother, Freud. As alpha, Frodo ruled with strength and authority. He protected his family, led them on hunts, and competed fiercely for mates.

Frodo was a big chimp, weighing over 120 pounds (55 kilograms), making him larger and stronger than most of the other chimps. Despite his tough demeanor, Frodo had a softer side too. He cared deeply for his family and fathered many offspring, ensuring the future of his chimpanzee lineage.

One of Frodo's most remarkable traits was his determination. Even when faced with challenges and illness, Frodo remained resilient. After being deposed as alpha in 2003 due to sickness, Frodo spent time recovering on his own. He returned to his community with a new perspective, showing less aggression and more wisdom.

Throughout his life, Frodo was a star in the eyes of researchers and filmmakers. He appeared in documentaries and films that showcased his remarkable journey as a chimpanzee leader. People from around the world admired Frodo for his strength, resilience, and unique personality.

Sadly, Frodo's story came to an end on November 10, 2013. His passing left a void in Gombe National Park, where he had ruled for many years. But Frodo's legacy lives on through his offspring and the memories of those who studied and admired him.

Frodo taught us many things about chimpanzees—about leadership, strength, and the complexities of life in the wild. His story reminds us that even in the animal kingdom, there are remarkable individuals with stories worth telling and lessons worth learning.

Saving Chimpanzees and Communities

In 1977, Jane Goodall started something amazing called the Jane Goodall Institute (JGI). This institute helps with the research happening in Gombe and works to protect chimpanzees and their homes. JGI has offices all over the world—nineteen of them! They are known for helping communities in Africa protect their natural resources and develop in a way that keeps the environment healthy.

One special program started by JGI is called Roots & Shoots. It began in 1991 when 16 local teenagers met Jane on her back porch in Tanzania. They talked about problems they cared deeply about, like helping animals and keeping the Earth clean. Now, there are over 10,000 Roots & Shoots groups in more than 100 countries! Kids everywhere are working together to make the world a better place.

In 1992, Jane opened the Tchimpounga Chimpanzee Rehabilitation Centre in the Republic of Congo. This place takes care of chimpanzees who lost their families because of hunting for bush meat. The center has helped more than a hundred chimps find safety and care on its three islands.

Two years later, in 1994, Jane started another important project called TACARE (Take Care). This project focuses on protecting the habitat of chimpanzees around Gombe by planting trees in the hills and teaching nearby communities about how to take care of their environment. TACARE also helps young girls by teaching them about their health and offering scholarships to help them go to college.

Jane Goodall's work with the Jane Goodall Institute and these amazing projects shows us how we can all make a difference for animals and our planet. She believes that when people come together and care for nature, we can create a better world for everyone.

ERIC LYLANI

Preserving Knowledge and Protecting Nature

In the mid-1990s, Jane Goodall's home in Dar es Salaam became filled with handwritten notes, photographs, and piles of data from her years of studying chimpanzees. To help organize all this important information, the Jane Goodall Institute's Center for Primate Studies was created at the University of Minnesota. This special center stored and organized Jane's archives, turning handwritten notes into digital records that could be easily accessed online.

By 2011, all of Jane Goodall's original archives were safely stored at the University of Minnesota and made available in a digital database for scientists and researchers around the world to study.

In 2011, the archives moved to Duke University under the care of Anne E. Pusey, an expert in evolutionary anthropology who had worked with Jane in Tanzania. Anne oversaw the collection, ensuring that Jane's valuable research would continue to be preserved and studied.

In more recent years, Jane Goodall has teamed up with her friend and CEO, Michael Cammarata, to create natural product lines with Schmidt's Naturals and Neptune Wellness Solutions. Five percent of every sale from these products goes to support the Jane Goodall Institute's important work protecting chimpanzees and their habitats.

Since 2004, Jane has devoted most of her time to advocating for chimpanzees and the environment. She travels almost 300 days a year, spreading awareness about the importance of conservation.

Jane is also an advisory board member for Save the Chimps, the world's largest chimpanzee sanctuary outside of Africa, located in Fort Pierce, Florida. She plays a key role in ensuring that chimpanzees in sanctuaries receive the care and respect they deserve.

Additionally, Jane Goodall serves as an advisory board member for The Society for the Protection of Underground Networks (SPUN), showing her commitment to protecting all kinds of wildlife and habitats, both above and below the ground.

Jane Goodall's lifelong dedication to chimpanzees and the environment inspires people everywhere to take action and make a positive difference for our planet and all its inhabitants.

Champion for Animals and the Environment

Jane Goodall has always been a passionate advocate for animals and our planet. In 1986, she attended the Understanding Chimpanzees conference in Chicago, which changed her focus from simply observing chimpanzees to a deeper concern for conservation. This shift inspired Jane to work tirelessly to protect animals and their habitats.

As the former president of Advocates for Animals in Scotland, Jane campaigned against using animals in medical research, zoos, farming, and sport. She strongly believed that animals deserve respect and kindness and spoke out against the mistreatment of farm animals used for food.

Jane is a vegetarian and later became a vegan in 2021. She promotes this diet for ethical, environmental, and health reasons, believing that animals deserve better treatment than they often receive in the food industry.

Jane is also an environmental advocate, speaking out about the impact of climate change on endangered species like chimpanzees. She partnered with NASA to use satellite imagery to help communities in Africa protect their forests and preserve wildlife habitats.

To ensure animals are treated ethically in scientific studies, Jane co-founded

Ethologists for the Ethical Treatment of Animals with Professor Mark Bekoff in 2000.

In 2008, Jane gave a lecture called "Reason for Hope," sharing her optimism about the future of our planet. She has been a strong voice urging the European Union to end animal testing and invest in alternative research methods.

Although Jane once praised a zoo enclosure, she later resigned from her role as president of an animal advocacy organization, citing her busy schedule. Despite this, she remains dedicated to supporting charities like Population Matters and working with Disneynature to raise awareness about nature conservation.

ERIC LYLANI

Voice for the Voiceless

In 2010, Jane Goodall and her institute, the Jane Goodall Institute (JGI), teamed up with other organizations like the Wildlife Conservation Society and the Humane Society of the United States. Together, they asked the government to protect all chimpanzees, even those in captivity, by listing them as endangered animals. This would help make sure that all chimpanzees are safe and cared for.

Five years later, in 2015, the US Fish and Wildlife Service agreed with their request. They decided that all chimpanzees should be classified as endangered to keep them safe from harm.

Jane Goodall has always cared deeply about animals. In 2011, she became a patron of Voiceless, an animal protection group in Australia. She spoke out against factory farming, where animals are raised in large numbers in small spaces, causing harm to the environment and suffering to the animals.

In 2012, Jane took on a new challenge called the Engage in Conservation Challenge. She worked with a group of young people who wanted to make a difference in protecting nature. Together, they created workshops to teach others about conserving biodiversity and why it's so important.

Jane also wrote letters to Air France and the National Institutes of Health (NIH) to speak up for animals. She criticized Air France for transporting monkeys to laboratories and spoke out against experiments that separated baby monkeys from their mothers.

Before the UK general election in 2015, Jane supported a candidate from the Green Party who cared about protecting animals and nature. She's also against fox hunting and signed a letter to lawmakers opposing changes to laws that protect foxes from being hunted.

In 2019, Jane was honored with a bronze sculpture in New York City for her contributions to science. She continues to advocate for the environment and animals. In 2020, she pledged to plant 5 million trees to help combat climate change and the destruction of nature.

In 2021, Jane joined the Rewriting Extinction campaign, using comics to raise awareness about the climate and biodiversity crisis. She believes that everyone can play a part in saving our planet and the animals that call it home.

A Tale of Love and Dedication

Jane Goodall has had two marriages. Her first marriage took place on March 28, 1964, at Chelsea Old Church in London. She married Baron Hugo van Lawick, a Dutch nobleman and wildlife photographer. During their marriage, Jane was known as Baroness Jane van Lawick-Goodall. Together, they had a son named Hugo Eric Louis, who was born in 1967.

Baron Hugo van Lawick was a renowned wildlife filmmaker and photographer who captured stunning images of chimpanzees and other wildlife in Africa. He and Jane worked closely together, with Hugo documenting Jane's groundbreaking research on chimpanzee behavior at Gombe Stream National Park in Tanzania. Their partnership contributed greatly to our understanding of chimpanzees and their natural habitat.

Unfortunately, Jane and Baron Hugo van Lawick divorced in 1974, but they remained connected through their shared passion for wildlife conservation and their son, Hugo.

After her divorce, Jane married Derek Bryceson in the following year. Derek was not only a member of Tanzania's parliament but also the director of the country's national parks. His position allowed him to support Jane's research efforts and protect her project at Gombe from tourism impacts.

Derek Bryceson played a crucial role in conservation efforts in Tanzania, advocating for the protection of wildlife and their habitats. Tragically, Derek passed away from cancer in October 1980, leaving behind a legacy of dedication to environmental preservation.

Throughout her life, Jane Goodall has expressed a deep love for animals, particularly dogs, which she considers her favorite animal companions. Despite facing challenges like prosopagnosia, a condition that makes it difficult to recognize familiar faces, Jane's unwavering passion for wildlife and conservation has inspired people around the world to protect and cherish our natural world.

The Feeding Station Controversy

When Jane Goodall studied chimpanzees in Gombe Stream National Park, she faced challenges from other scientists who questioned her methods. Some scientists thought that using feeding stations to attract the chimpanzees changed their behavior. Margaret Power wrote a book in 1991 saying that feeding stations caused more fighting and disagreements among the chimpanzee groups in the area.

They thought that the feeding might have caused what Jane Goodall called "wars" between the chimpanzees' social groups, something she hadn't seen before starting the feeding. This made some scientists wonder if Jane's observations really showed how wild chimpanzees behave naturally.

Jane Goodall agreed that feeding might make the chimpanzees act more aggressive. But she believed that the feeding only made their fights more intense, not different in kind. She thought that using feeding stations was important to study the chimpanzees properly.

Craig Stanford, from the Jane Goodall Research Institute, explained that it's hard for researchers without feeding stations to see how chimpanzees act socially, especially when they are arguing or fighting with each other.

Other scientists, like Crickette Sanz and Christophe Boesch, studied chimpanzees in different places without using feeding stations and didn't see the same fights that Jane saw at Gombe. However, some researchers didn't agree that feeding stations made a big difference to the studies. Jim Moore disagreed with Margaret Power's ideas, and studies of other chimpanzee groups showed similar fights even without feeding.

Studying wild animals like chimpanzees is tricky, and scientists use different ways to understand how they act in their natural homes. Each study teaches us more about these amazing animals and how they live in the wild.

ERIC LYLANI

Seeds of Hope

In March 2013, Jane Goodall's eagerly anticipated book, "Seeds of Hope," co-authored with Gail Hudson, was set for release on April 2. However, there was an unexpected delay.

Despite this setback, "Seeds of Hope" emerged as a significant work exploring the importance of plants and their impact on human life and the environment. This insightful book delves into topics such as biodiversity, sustainable agriculture, and the interconnectedness of life on Earth.

Goodall and Hudson highlight the critical role that plants play in sustaining ecosystems and supporting life. Through engaging narratives and scientific insights, they unveil the mysteries of plants and their incredible potential to heal our bodies and our planet.

"Seeds of Hope" takes readers on a journey from England to Africa, deep within the Gombe forest, where Goodall and the chimpanzees are captivated by fig and plum trees. Along the way, she introduces botanists from around the globe and shares stories of places filled with hope for plants, like The Millennium Seed Bank.

Viewing the world through the lens of an adventurer, scientist, and advocate of sustainable living, Goodall presents simple steps that we can all take to protect the plants in our own environments.

In her wise and elegant new book, "Seeds of Hope," Jane Goodall blends her lifelong experience in nature with her passion for botany to offer readers a deeper understanding of the world around us. Through this enlightening exploration, she encourages us to discover the magic of nature right in our own backyards.

ERIC LYLANI

Awards and Recognition

Jane Goodall has received numerous awards and honors for her incredible work in the fields of environmental conservation and humanitarian efforts.

One of her notable recognitions came in 2004 when she was named a Dame Commander of the Order of the British Empire at Buckingham Palace. This prestigious honor acknowledged her remarkable contributions to science and conservation.

In 2002, United Nations Secretary-General Kofi Annan appointed Goodall as a United

Nations Messenger of Peace, recognizing her dedication to promoting peace and protecting the planet.

Among her many awards, Goodall has been honored with the Tyler Prize for Environmental Achievement, the French Legion of Honour, and Tanzania's Medal of Honor. She also received Japan's esteemed Kyoto Prize, the Benjamin Franklin Medal in Life Science, and the Gandhi-King Award for Nonviolence, highlighting her global impact and dedication to positive change.

Jane Goodall's influence extends to popular culture, as she is honored with a plaque on the Tree of Life at Disney's Animal Kingdom theme park. The plaque commemorates her groundbreaking research and features a carving of David Greybeard, the chimpanzee who first approached her during her studies at Gombe.

She holds memberships in prestigious institutions like the American Academy of Arts and Sciences and the American Philosophical Society, reflecting her profound impact on scientific and philosophical communities.

In 2010, Dave Matthews and Tim Reynolds held a benefit concert to celebrate "Gombe 50," marking the 50th anniversary of Goodall's pioneering research with chimpanzees.

Time magazine recognized her as one of the 100 most influential people in the world in 2019, further underscoring her global influence and legacy.

In 2021, she was awarded the Templeton Prize, a testament to her significant contributions to understanding human spirituality and the interconnectedness of life.

Recently, in 2022, Jane Goodall received the Stephen Hawking Medal for Science Communication in recognition of her groundbreaking research on the social and family interactions of wild chimpanzees.

Continuing her streak of honors, in April 2023, she was appointed Officer in the Order of Orange-Nassau in a ceremony held in The Hague, the Netherlands, highlighting her international impact and ongoing dedication to conservation efforts.

Exploring Gombe

Imagine venturing deep into the lush jungles of Tanzania, armed with curiosity and determination. That's exactly what Dr. Jane Goodall did in 1960 when she embarked on her groundbreaking research with chimpanzees at Gombe National Park.

At the young age of 26, Jane was sent to Tanzania by Dr. Louis Leakey, a renowned anthropologist. Her mission: to study the mysterious lives of chimpanzees in their natural habitat. But Jane wasn't alone; her mother, Vanne, joined her for support and companionship.

Gombe National Park sits along the shores of Lake Tanganyika, bordering Burundi and the Congo. The dense forests and steep valleys provided a challenging backdrop for Jane's research.

Jane's early days at Gombe were filled with frustration. The chimpanzees kept their distance, making it difficult for her to observe their behaviors. Despite her efforts, Jane could not get closer than 50 yards to the curious primates.

To make matters worse, Jane and her mother fell ill with malaria. Bedridden and weak, they battled the illness with the help of their guide, David, who urged them to seek medical attention.

One day, a curious male chimpanzee approached their camp, eyeing a banana on the table. This encounter gave Jane an idea. She began leaving bananas nearby, attracting the chimps and earning their trust.

Gradually, the chimpanzees allowed Jane to follow them as they foraged and interacted. They even greeted her with touches and kisses, showcasing a growing bond of trust.

One pivotal moment came when Jane observed a male chimp, later named David Greybeard, eating a baby bush pig—a surprising revelation. Chimpanzees were thought to be herbivores, but this discovery challenged that belief. Jane's observations reshaped our understanding of primate behavior.

Excited by her findings, Jane shared her discoveries with Dr. Louis Leakey, who immediately arranged for additional funding and support. National Geographic joined her study in 1964, documenting her groundbreaking research.

Despite facing criticism from some in the scientific community for her unconventional methods, Jane remained committed to her work. She earned her Ph.D. from Cambridge University in 1965, becoming one of the few to do so without a bachelor's degree.

Jane's journey teaches us the importance of perseverance and thinking outside the box. Her discoveries revolutionized our understanding of chimpanzees and paved the way for future research in primatology.

Exploring the Great Apes

In this chapter, we'll embark on a journey to discover the similarities and differences among some of our closest relatives in the animal kingdom: chimpanzees, gorillas, orangutans, and bonobos.

Chimpanzees are highly intelligent and social creatures known for their problem-solving abilities and complex social behaviors. They live in communities led by an alpha male and form strong bonds with family members. Chimpanzees use tools, such as sticks, to fish out termites from mounds, showcasing their advanced cognitive skills.

Gorillas, on the other hand, are the gentle giants of the jungle. They live in family groups led by a dominant silverback male. Gorillas are herbivores and spend much of their time foraging for leaves, fruits, and shoots. Unlike chimpanzees, gorillas are more solitary and less likely to use tools extensively.

Moving to orangutans, these majestic creatures are the largest arboreal (tree-dwelling) animals on Earth. They have a striking reddish-brown coat and are known for their long, powerful arms. Orangutans are solitary creatures, with males having large cheek pads called flanges. They are highly intelligent and have been observed using tools like sticks to extract food.

Bonobos are closely related to chimpanzees and share many physical features. However, they are known for their peaceful and egalitarian social structure.

All great apes, including humans, share a significant amount of DNA, highlighting our evolutionary connections. They are highly social and form complex family groups, exhibiting emotions such as empathy, cooperation, and mourning for their deceased members. Great apes demonstrate high levels of intelligence, problem-solving abilities, and capacity for learning. They communicate through vocalizations, gestures, and facial expressions, each species having its own unique ways of expressing emotions and conveying information.

Despite their similarities, great apes also exhibit differences in physical characteristics, social behavior, and habitat preferences. Gorillas are more solitary compared to chimpanzees and bonobos, which live in larger social groups. Each species inhabits different regions of Africa and Southeast Asia, adapting to diverse environments from dense rainforests to mountainous terrains. While all great apes use tools to some extent, chimpanzees are known for their sophisticated tool-making behaviors, using objects like stones and sticks for various purposes.

Unfortunately, all great ape species are endangered or critically endangered due to habitat loss, poaching, and diseases. Conservation efforts are crucial to protect these magnificent creatures and ensure their survival in the wild.

Fascinating Facts about Chimpanzees

In the heart of Africa, deep within lush tropical forests, lives a remarkable creature - the chimpanzee.

Picture a chimpanzee: They have long arms that extend below their knees, short legs, and bodies covered in black hair. Their faces are expressive, with big eyes, a small nose, and a wide mouth. Chimpanzees are incredibly similar to humans, sharing 98.5% of our DNA!

Chimpanzees make their homes in the tropical forests and woodland savannahs of West and Central Africa. Their populations are spread across different countries, with the largest groups found in places like Gabon, the Democratic Republic of Congo, and Cameroon. These forests provide chimps with everything they need to survive – from food to shelter.

Chimpanzees are social animals and live in communities led by a dominant alpha male. These communities can range in size from 15 to 80 members! Within their groups, chimpanzees form smaller sub-groups that sleep, travel, and feed together. Each chimp has its own unique personality and plays a role in the community.

Did you know that chimpanzees are incredibly intelligent? They're the second-most intelligent primates after humans!

Chimpanzees communicate with each other using gestures, facial expressions, and various vocalizations like hoots, grunts and screams. They have complex ways of interacting and expressing emotions.

Chimpanzees are omnivores, which means they eat a variety of foods. Their favorite meal is fruits, but they also enjoy leaves, flowers, seeds, bird eggs, insects, and even small animals like monkeys and wild pigs! Some groups of chimpanzees have been known to consume up to 200 different kinds of food.

One of the most impressive things about chimpanzees is their ability to use tools. They crack open nuts using rocks, fish out insects from nests with sticks, and even fashion leaves into makeshift umbrellas to shield themselves from rain. This shows just how clever and resourceful they are!

Chimpanzees have close family bonds. Female chimps give birth to a single baby chimp (or occasionally twins) every five to six years. For the first six months of their lives, babies cling to their mother's belly. After that, they ride on their mother's back until they're around two years old. Young chimps spend many years with their mothers, learning essential survival skills.

Chimpanzees face serious threats in the wild. Their habitats are being destroyed due to deforestation, and they're hunted for bushmeat. They're also captured for use in zoos, circuses, and medical research. Because of these dangers, their populations are declining, and they're now classified as endangered.

Fortunately, there are people and organizations working hard to protect chimpanzees. Conservationists are creating protected areas where chimps can live safely. They're also raising awareness about the importance of preserving forests and stopping the illegal wildlife trade. By supporting these efforts, we can help ensure a future where chimpanzees continue to thrive in the wild.

Chimpanzees are not just fascinating creatures – they're our closest relatives in the animal kingdom. Their intelligence, social behaviors, and remarkable adaptability inspire us to appreciate and protect the natural world. Let's celebrate the wonder of chimpanzees and join hands to ensure a bright future for these amazing animals!

ERIC LYLANI

Peacekeeping Among Primates

In the lush forests of Africa where chimpanzees swing from tree to tree, there exists a complex world of social interactions. Chimpanzees, like humans, sometimes face disagreements and conflicts within their groups. How do these clever creatures navigate these challenges?

Dr. Jane Goodall spent decades studying our closest relatives, the chimpanzees, in their natural habitat. One of the intriguing aspects of her research was uncovering how chimpanzees manage conflicts to maintain peace in their communities.

Chimpanzees, much like us, have various strategies for resolving disagreements. One of the most important ways they promote harmony is through grooming. Grooming involves picking through each other's fur to remove dirt and parasites. This may seem like a simple act, but it plays a crucial role in chimpanzee social life. When two chimpanzees groom each other, it helps to strengthen their bond and reduce tension after a disagreement.

Imagine a chimpanzee named Frodo who had a dispute with another male over a tasty fruit. After the disagreement, Frodo approached the other male and gently started grooming his back. This act of grooming signaled to the other chimpanzee that Frodo wanted to make amends and restore their friendship.

Another way chimpanzees resolve conflicts is through vocalizations. Chimpanzees have a diverse range of calls, including hoots, grunts, and screams. During disputes, they may use vocalizations to express their emotions and intentions. Sometimes, a loud display of vocalizations can diffuse a tense situation by asserting dominance or signaling submission.

Jane Goodall noticed that certain vocalizations helped chimpanzees communicate their feelings during conflicts. For instance, when two males were vying for the same female's attention, one of them would emit a series of deep, powerful hoots to assert dominance and intimidate the other male.

Dominance displays are also common among chimpanzees. When conflicts arise, dominant individuals may use body language to establish their authority and restore order. This can include puffing up their chests, standing tall, or even charging at others to show strength.

One memorable example from Jane Goodall's research involved a conflict between two rival males over access to a termite mound. As tensions escalated, the dominant male charged at the other, causing him to retreat and avoid further confrontation. Through these displays, chimpanzees establish a social hierarchy that helps prevent continuous conflicts.

Jane Goodall's groundbreaking research showed that conflict resolution among chimpanzees involves a complex interplay of behaviors aimed at maintaining social cohesion. By studying these behaviors, Dr. Goodall provided valuable insights into the social dynamics of our primate cousins.

Chimpanzees, much like humans, employ a range of strategies to resolve conflicts within their groups. From grooming and vocalizations to displays of dominance, these behaviors play essential roles in maintaining peace and harmony in chimpanzee communities. Thanks to Jane Goodall's meticulous observations, we have gained a deeper understanding of how chimpanzees navigate social challenges and forge relationships in the wild.

ERIC LYLANI

Chimpanzee Family Bonds

Chimpanzees, like humans, have strong family bonds that shape their lives. Jane Goodall spent years observing these incredible creatures, documenting their behaviors and relationships.

One of Jane's most exciting discoveries was the close bond between mother and child among chimpanzees. Just like human mothers, chimpanzee mothers care for their young with tenderness and patience. Jane witnessed mothers cradling their babies, grooming them, and providing them with nourishment and protection. This loving care helps young chimpanzees grow up strong and healthy.

Imagine Jane quietly watching as a mother chimpanzee named Flo held her baby, Fifi, close to her chest. Flo gently groomed Fifi's fur, removing dirt and parasites. Fifi, in turn, clung tightly to her mother, feeling safe and secure in her embrace. Jane marveled at the tender moments shared between mother and child in the chimpanzee world.

Sibling relationships are also essential among chimpanzees. Just like human brothers and sisters, chimpanzee siblings play together and support each other. Jane observed young chimpanzees chasing each other through the trees, wrestling playfully, and sharing food. These playful interactions strengthen their bonds and teach them valuable social skills.

In one of Jane's observations, she witnessed two chimpanzee siblings, Freud and Fifi, engaging in a playful wrestling match. Freud, the older brother, allowed Fifi to climb on his back and swing from his arms. Their playful antics brought joy to Jane's heart as she realized how similar chimpanzee siblings are to human children.

Chimpanzees also exhibit cooperative behaviors within their families. Older siblings often help care for younger siblings, grooming them and sharing food. This cooperation fosters a sense of unity and support within the chimpanzee community.

Jane Goodall's research shed light on the deep emotional connections that exist within chimpanzee families. She showed us that these remarkable creatures experience love, care, and companionship, much like our own families.

Chimpanzees form strong family bonds characterized by nurturing mothers, playful siblings, and cooperative behaviors. Thanks to Jane Goodall's groundbreaking work, we have gained valuable insights into the intricate social lives of chimpanzees. Through her observations, Jane revealed the beauty and complexity of chimpanzee family dynamics, highlighting the similarities between humans and our closest relatives in the animal kingdom.

Decoding Chimp Language

In the lush forests of Gombe, Jane Goodall listened closely to the voices of the chimpanzees. These clever creatures had a language all their own, and Jane was determined to understand it.

Chimpanzees are like us in many ways, and one of the most fascinating similarities is how they communicate. They use a combination of sounds, gestures, and facial expressions to express themselves. Just like when you smile to show you're happy or frown when you're upset, chimpanzees have their own ways of sharing feelings.

One of the most common sounds you might hear in the chimpanzee world is a pant-hoot. This loud call echoes through the trees and can mean different things depending on how it's used. Sometimes, it's a joyful greeting between friends. Other times, it's a warning to stay away!

Chimpanzees also use gestures to communicate. They might reach out a hand to ask for food or groom a friend to show affection. Jane noticed that chimpanzees could even use objects like sticks to communicate, tapping them on trees to make noise.

One special chimpanzee named David Greybeard taught Jane something incredible. He was the first chimpanzee she saw using tools, like a stick to fish for termites. This showed Jane that chimpanzees were not just smart, but they could also teach each other new ways to do things.

Through her studies, Jane discovered that chimpanzees have rich emotional lives. They laugh when they play and comfort each other when they're scared. They can even argue, just like we do!

By paying close attention to how chimpanzees talk to each other, Jane Goodall opened up a whole new world of understanding. She showed us that these amazing animals have their own language of love, anger, and friendship, and it's a language worth listening to.

Exploring Chimpanzee Cuisine

In the lush forests of Africa, among the towering trees and dense undergrowth, chimpanzees lead fascinating lives filled with adventure and discovery. But what do these intelligent primates eat, and how do they find their food?

Jane Goodall has revealed some incredible insights into their feeding habits.

Chimpanzees are not picky eaters. They have diverse diets that include a wide range of foods. Imagine waking up in the morning and deciding whether to munch on juicy fruits, tender leaves, or crunchy insects—chimpanzees face these choices every day!

Fruits are a favorite among chimpanzees. They feast on a variety of fruits they find in the forest, from figs and berries to wild plums and papayas. Chimpanzees are clever at finding ripe fruits and often use their strong hands to pluck them from trees.

But their diet doesn't stop at fruits. Chimpanzees also enjoy munching on leaves and leafy greens. They carefully select which leaves to eat, preferring the tender ones that are easier to chew.

Insects are another tasty treat for chimpanzees. They skillfully use sticks or twigs to fish out insects from nests or tree crevices. Ants and termites are particularly delicious snacks that chimpanzees love to savor.

One surprising aspect of chimpanzees' diets is their occasional taste for meat. Yes, you heard that right! While chimpanzees are mainly vegetarians, they sometimes hunt and eat small mammals like monkeys. Jane Goodall's groundbreaking discovery of this behavior shows just how adaptable and opportunistic chimpanzees can be when it comes to finding food.

Chimpanzees are true opportunistic feeders, meaning they take advantage of whatever food is available in their environment. They use their keen senses and clever problem-solving skills to locate and extract food from various sources, adapting to changes in seasons and availability.

Thanks to Jane Goodall's tireless efforts and keen observations, we now have a deeper understanding of the diverse and resourceful feeding habits of these amazing animals. The next time you enjoy a snack, think about the chimpanzees swinging through the treetops and exploring the forest for their next delicious meal!

A Mission To Protect Chimpanzees

One of the biggest threats to chimpanzees is the illegal pet trade. Chimpanzees are often captured from the wild when they are young and sold as exotic pets. This not only disrupts their natural social structures but also puts them at risk of abuse and neglect. Jane has worked tirelessly to raise awareness about the cruelty of the pet trade and to advocate for laws that protect chimpanzees from being exploited in this way.

Another major concern is the use of chimpanzees in medical research.

Chimpanzees share more than 98% of their DNA with humans, making them valuable subjects for scientific study. However, this has led to their exploitation in laboratories, where they may be subjected to invasive experiments that cause them pain and suffering. Jane has been a vocal critic of using chimpanzees in research and has campaigned for more ethical alternatives.

Habitat loss is also a significant threat to chimpanzees. As human populations grow, forests are cleared for agriculture, logging, and development, shrinking the available habitat for chimpanzees. This loss of habitat not only reduces the space where chimpanzees can live but also disrupts their access to food and resources. Jane has worked to establish protected areas like Gombe Stream National Park to provide a safe haven for chimpanzees and other wildlife.

The ongoing struggle to protect chimpanzees can be difficult for Jane and others who care deeply about these animals. It is heartbreaking to see chimpanzees suffer due to human actions, and Jane has faced many challenges in her efforts to ensure their well-being. Despite the sadness and frustration, Jane remains determined to speak out for chimpanzees and to inspire others to join her in the fight to protect these incredible creatures.

ERIC LYLANI

Lessons from Jane Goodall

Imagine yourself deep in the African jungle, surrounded by curious chimpanzees and the lush sounds of nature. This was the world of Jane Goodall—a world she discovered through passion, dedication, and a relentless pursuit of her dreams.

Jane's journey began with a deep curiosity about animals and the natural world. She encourages you to ask questions, explore new ideas, and stay curious about the world around you. When you're curious, you'll find the motivation to learn and discover new passions.

Follow your heart and pursue what truly excites you, even if it's different from what others expect. Don't be afraid to forge your own path and embrace your unique interests and talents.

Success doesn't come overnight. Jane spent years observing and studying chimpanzees, facing challenges and setbacks along the way. She teaches us the importance of hard work, persistence, and resilience. Keep pushing forward, even when things get tough, and never give up on your dreams.

Educate yourself continuously. Stay curious, read books, watch documentaries, and seek out mentors who can guide you on your journey. Knowledge and expertise will empower you to pursue your dreams with confidence.

Take action and make a difference in the world. Whether you volunteer at a wildlife sanctuary, participate in conservation projects, or raise awareness about environmental issues, find ways to contribute to causes you care about.

Develop key skills such as observation, critical thinking, communication, and empathy. These skills will not only help you in your studies but also prepare you for a meaningful career in conservation or animal behavior research.

Spending time in nature can be transformative. Jane encourages you to connect with the natural world, whether it's exploring local parks, observing wildlife, or simply taking walks outdoors. Nature has a way of inspiring creativity and nurturing a sense of wonder.

Be patient and flexible with your goals. Sometimes, unexpected opportunities or challenges may arise, leading you down a different path. Embrace these experiences and stay open to new possibilities.

Above all, believe in yourself and your abilities. Trust that you have the power to make a positive impact on the world. Set goals, work hard, and never stop believing in your dreams.

If you dream of a career like Jane Goodall's, remember that it requires dedication, passion, and a lifelong commitment to learning and conservation. Start by studying hard, exploring your interests, and taking small steps toward your goals. With determination and perseverance, you can turn your dreams into reality and make a meaningful difference in the world, just like Jane Goodall did.

CONCLUSION

As we reach the end of this captivating journey through the life and work of Jane Goodall, one thing becomes clear: passion, dedication, and love for nature can truly change the world.

Jane's story is not just about studying chimpanzees; it's about the profound connection between humans and the natural world. Through her experiences, we've learned the importance of conservation, empathy for all living beings, and the power of perseverance in the face of challenges.

Jane Goodall's legacy inspires us to be stewards of our planet, to protect wildlife and their habitats, and to advocate for a more sustainable future. Her work reminds us that each of us has the ability to make a difference, no matter how big or small.

As we bid farewell to this book, let's carry forward Jane's message of hope, resilience, and compassion. Let's continue to ask questions, seek knowledge, and take action to preserve the incredible diversity of life on Earth.

Thank you for joining us on this adventure. Remember, the journey to protect our planet is ongoing, and together, we can create a brighter future for all species, including our closest relatives, the chimpanzees.

Keep exploring, keep learning, and never stop being curious.

Goodbye for now, and may you be inspired to follow your dreams just as Jane Goodall did.

ERIC LYLANI

Made in the USA
Las Vegas, NV
08 October 2024

96407611R20069